# EMOTIONAL INTELLGENCE

**A Practical Guide on How to Improve Your Emotional Intelligence, Be Smart in Life, Earn Greater Rewards and Live Happily**

# BOOK DESCRIPTION

This book is a guide that provides you with information on emotional intelligence (EI) and hands-on practical steps to improve your emotional intelligence so that you can live a better quality of life.

The guide employs a beginners' approach by starting off with what emotional intelligence is. This enables you to have an in-depth understanding on emotional intelligence. It further goes on to explore the difference between Emotional Quotient (EQ) and general Intelligence Quotient (IQ), which are simply standard measures of emotional intelligence and general intelligence, respectively.

Benefits of emotional intelligence are immense and infinite. Nonetheless, this book has explored some of the most important benefits that you will derive should you work to improve your emotional intelligence. To enable you to have a better perspective on these benefits, the book provides real life scenarios in which emotional intelligence or lack of it plays a critical role. With these examples, you can easily relate emotional intelligence to your own everyday situations.

The greatest challenge that faces many is how to test their emotional intelligence so that they can estimate the magnitude of improvement required. There are many tools that have emerged to help one measure his/her own EQ. Sadly, due to huge interest in emotional intelligence, some tools have been developed hastily to meet this insatiable demand. Consequently, some are not empirically proven. This guide has listed those tools which have been scientifically proven as appropriate measures of EQ. This will help you to more accurately measure your EQ level.

Once you have determined your EQ level, it is naturally obvious that, regardless of outcome, you would desire to improve on it. The advantage of EQ is that it is elastic and dynamic. Thus, no matter your level of EQ, there is always room for improvement. In this regard, this guide has endeavored to provide you with most impactful techniques and tips that you can apply to boost your emotional intelligence.

Having a great emotional intelligence and retaining the same level of EQ is a daily lifetime endeavor. Thus, you need to have a routine that will enable you to be disciplined enough to be on track. Hence, this book has provided 30 daily habits which you can practice to improve your emotional intelligence.

Enjoy your reading.

# GIFT INCLUDED

If you are an entrepreneur, an aspiring entrepreneur, someone who is trying to create additional income stream, or even someone who just loves self improvement books; then you need to read my recommendations for top 10 business books ever.

# ABOUT THE AUTHOR

George Pain is an entrepreneur, author and business consultant. He specializes in setting up online businesses from scratch, investment income strategies and global mobility solutions. He has built several businesses from the ground up, and is excited to share his knowledge with readers.

# DISCLAIMER

# CONTENTS

# INTRODUCTION

Emotional intelligence has emerged as one of the most important traits we need for success in life.

People with extremely high IQ (Intelligence Quotient) becoming society's intellectual derelicts is more than just a proverb. Societies has always been concerned with why a significant proportion of people. who were considered great intellectuals, ended up becoming social misfits, alcoholics and drug abusers. This weird situation prompted various studies on this issue. One of these great studies came up with the discovery that, contrary to our traditional knowledge of intelligence, there is not just one but multiple types of intelligence. Another study conduced by Goleman found out that emotional intelligence (EI) contributed to about 75% of success in life.

Unfortunately, our education system still remains traditional and more academic-oriented. Thus, the syllabus is largely geared towards general intelligence, sometimes referred to as mental intelligence. This has meant that most people graduate high on IQ optimization and less on EQ (Emotional Quotient) optimization. This leaves people to work on their own to boost their EQ. Lately, employers, have taken up the challenge of teaching people EI. However, studies have also found that EI is relevant in schooling as it is a catalyst for better application of one's general intelligence. Thus, it is not only important for those who are already out of school to start working on their emotional intelligence, but also parents and teachers to start helping students improve on their emotional intelligence.

This book is geared towards informing, sensitizing and enabling our society to improve on their emotional intelligence. This will not only make people perform better in their personal and collective endeavors, but, will also help to bring down rates of social delinquency due to behaviors as binge eating, alcoholism, drug abuse, crime etc. A nation can save billions of dollars by simply increasing the levels of emotional intelligence in society.

I hope you will be richly endowed with the information provided in this book and successfully work towards improving your emotional intelligence.


Keep reading!

Thank you.

# WHAT IS EMOTIONAL INTELLIGENCE?

Scientists over time have come to the conclusion that, despite earlier findings, that we humans don't have one but several uniquely different sets of intelligence.

Most scientists concur that we have the following main sets of intelligence.

1. Mental intelligence
2. Emotional intelligence
3. Social intelligence

Though not universally agreed, there are those others who add the following extra sets of intelligence;

4. Psychological intelligence
5. Spiritual intelligence

It is commonly held that, apart from the traditionally known general intelligence, more specifically, mental intelligence, emotional intelligence is the second most important intelligence, if not the first. Yes, there is a new scientific school of thought which asserts that emotional intelligence is superior to mental intelligence.

Nonetheless, without dwelling further in the dispute as to which of these two is the superior form of intelligence, it is our aim to unravel what emotional intelligence is so that you can make your very own deductions.

## So, what is Emotional intelligence?

Emotional intelligence refers to one's capability to recognize one's own emotions and those of others; differentiate feelings and label them accordingly; and utilize this intelligence information to guide one's thinking, words and actions in such a manner that achieves one's goals.

Like other scientific constructs, Emotional Intelligence has its own various models that support its realm. However, the three most prominent models are:

1. Ability Model
2. Mixed Model
3. Trait Model

Out of these three models, the model that has won the greatest concurrence from scientific community is the Mixed Model which has been advanced by Daniel Goleman. Thus, we are going to dwell more on the Mixed Model.

## Why Models?

Scientifically, any construct must be testable and measurable. Models help to advance testability and measurability. That which is not tests and measured lacks scientific dimension and thus cannot be effectively utilized.

## Daniel Goleman's Mixed Model

Daniel Goleman asserts that Emotional Intelligence has 5 components, which, in this book, we will refer to as the 5 Components of Emotional Intelligence (5 EIs).

## The 5 components of emotional intelligence

The 5 key components of emotional intelligence are;

1. Self-Awareness

2. Self-Regulation

3. Motivation

4. Empathy

5. Social skills

## Self-Awareness

This refers to being aware of one's emotions. This has three stages;

- Recognition – this refers to recognizing one's emotions and their impact
- Assessment – this refers to knowing one's strengths and weaknesses
- Assurance – this is a strong sense of one's self-worth and capabilities. It is one's self-confidence

## Self-Regulation (self-management)

This refers to managing one's internal states, impulses and resources. It involves three critical steps;

- Control – Involves being in charge of disruptive impulses and their distressing effects such as anxiety and anger.

- Integrity – Involves maintaining standards and honesty

- Conscientiousness – Involves making deliberate and informed decisions devoid of impulses and taking responsibility for the decisions made.

- Adaptability - Is the ability to adjust to changing circumstances

- Innovation – Refers to being open to new ideas and information and adjusting accordingly

## Motivation (self-management)

- Initiative – This is readiness to seize new opportunities

- Drive – This is the energy to propel oneself to achieving own goals
- Optimism – Remaining positive despite setbacks
- Commitment – Being disciplined and focused towards achievement of set goals

**Empathy (social awareness)**

Empathy refers to a state of being aware of other people's feelings, needs and concerns. It has the following key dimensions;

- Political awareness – Reading a group's emotional and power dynamics.

- Understanding Others – Being cognizant of other people's feelings and perspectives and taking active interest in their concerns.

- Leveraging Diversity – Refers to cultivating opportunities through the differences in people. That is, taking the sum total of their differences.

- Developing others – Enabling others to achieve their highest aspirations

- Serving others – Uplifting others to achieve their needs

## Social Skills (relationship skills)

This refers to being adept in inducing desirable responses in others. It involves;

- Communication – Listening attentively. Being able to detect verbal and non-verbal cues for negative emotions, more so, anger and fear; to judge trustworthiness of others; and being able to send convincing responses.

- Building bonds – Nurturing constructive bonds.

- Collaboration and cooperation (team capabilities) – Working with others synergistically to achieve shared goals.

- Influence – Having persuasive power to achieve desired response from others.

- Change catalyst – Being able to trigger or manage change.

- Leadership – Optimizing the blend of the above-mentioned social skills to achieve set vision (mission and goals).

## Functional regrouping

Functional regrouping helps you to easily identify these 5 components based on their functions:

There are two ways to carry out functional regrouping

- **Recognition –vs- Regulation**
- **Intrapersonal –vs- Interpersonal**

## Recognition –vs- regulation

1. Recognition
   - Self-awareness
   - Social awareness
2. Regulation
   - Self management (self-regulation and motivation)
   - Relationship management (social skills)

## Intrapersonal –vs- Interpersonal

1. Intrapersonal intelligence
   - Self-awareness
   - Self-management
   - Self-motivation
2. Interpersonal intelligence
   - Social awareness
   - Social competence

## The four stages of Emotions

Emotions happen in stages, the following are the four main stages;

- Perceiving emotions – This is the first stage where the emotional signal is received and converted into interpretable form.

- Reasoning with emotions – This is the second stage in which the perceived emotion is synthesized (interrogated and thought out).

- Understanding emotions – This is the stage at which meaning is derived from the synthesized emotional information.

- Managing emotions – This stage involves response and control. In this stage feedback is given in such a manner that is intended to achieve a certain goal.

## Why is it important to have Emotional Intelligence?

Emotional intelligence is important in all spheres of our life. We need it to progress in careers, to have successful families and have lasting relationships.

Importance of EQ can be seen in the following situations;

- Survival – People with high EQ are found to live longer and happier lives than those with low EQ. This is mainly because they are less susceptible to stress and more adaptable to changing circumstances.

- Decision-making – Decision making is 50% dependent on IQ and 50% dependent on EQ. Thus, if two people with the same IQ level make decisions, the one with higher EQ level is more likely to make better decision as compared to the one with lower EQ.

- Boundary-setting – Boundary-setting is important in your private life just as it is in your public life. It is commonly said that people who don't set boundary limits become doormats for others to wipe off their shoes. This is true. People with higher EQ are able to set boundaries with whom they can entertain; why, when and to what extent. People with high IQ also set boundaries, but, they are often rigid or sometimes choose avoidance rather than boundaries. Boundary-setting is one of the mechanisms that enable one to filter out what is not necessary and embrace that which is. It is not necessarily about keeping someone off, but, more about choosing what you allow to affect you. So, the boundaries are more emotional rather than physical. This is the reason why people with high EQ have wide and diverse networks. They don't just keep someone out; but emotionally filter in that which is necessary and filter out that which is not. They just don't get worked up because someone said something unpleasant, or stop a relationship with such a person on that basis. But, they simply don't allow that unpleasant utterance work them up. They simply discard it.

- Communication – Communication experts asserts that communication is 70% body language. When you are speaking, the greatest impact of your speech is not so much what you say but about how you say it. Of course the speech must not sacrifice substance. In your speech, how you manipulate your vocals and how you gesture has a great impact on those that you address. One person can make a speech from a given script and the audience remains simply silent and bored (switching of listening). Another person can make a speech from the very same script and the audience gets moved to tears, or laughs, or claps and at the end of it receive a standing ovation. The difference is not the substance (what is said) since the script is the same. The difference is in how it is said (the body language). The greatest orators are masters of body language.

- Unity – People with higher EQ are known to easily master group's underlying political currents and thus harness them to rally the group members together. By being empathetic and compassionate, they are able to enable each member of the group feel cared for. This helps to resolve conflicts and glue the group together, thus, fostering unity.

## What are the signs of low emotional intelligence?

It is inspiring to know the importance of high emotional intelligence. However, if we can't determine whether we have high or low emotional intelligence, then we cannot improve ourselves.

Thus, it is important that we are able to observe telling signs that can inform us whether we or the people we relate with have low emotional intelligence. This would help to avoid unnecessary conflicts.

The following are telling signs of low emotional intelligence;

1. Getting involved in lots of arguments

2. Not understanding others' feelings

3. Thinking that others are too insensitive

4. Mentally blocking yourself from others' point of view

5. Blaming others for their mistakes

6. Inability to cope with emotionally-charged situation

7. Emotional outbursts

8. Difficulty maintaining friendships

9. Expressing inappropriate emotions

10. Non-adaptive tone to changes in emotional situations

11. Trivializing emotional expressions

12. Getting easily stressed by minor challenges

13. Lack of assertiveness

14. Limited emotional vocabulary

15. Quick to make assumptions and rigid in defending them

16. Holding grudges

17. Not being able to tell one's emotional triggers

18. Frequently feeling misunderstood

19. Getting easily offended

20. Blaming others for how they make one feel

21. Not getting angry when the situation demands (it doesn't necessily mean you get out of control)

22. Getting surprised when others express sensitivity to own comments or jokes

**Three levels of emotional intelligence;**

- Emotional sensitivity

- Emotional maturity

- Emotional competence

**Emotional competence refers to;**

- Being in control of one's emotional impulses

- High levels of self-confidence

- Being in control of one's ego

- Overcoming inferiority issues

**Emotional maturity refers to;**

- Being self-aware

- Uplifting the good in others

- Overcoming cravings for instant want satisfaction

- Being flexible and adaptable to changing circumstances

**Emotional sensitivity refers to;**

- Being able to effectively communicate one's emotions

- Understing limits of emotional arousal

- Being cognizant of interpersonal needs

- Compassion

**Characteristics of High EI person;**

- Freely expresses own feelings

- Not overwhelmed by negatively impulsive emotions

- Strikes an optimal balance between logic, reason and reality

- Independent, autonomous and self-reliant

- Has positive regard to other people's feelings

- Knows when to listen and when to talk

- Emotionally resilient

- Not immobilized by fear

- Not motivated by wealth, fame, power, status or approval

## Characteristics of Low EI person (supplementary)

- Lacks empathy and compassion

- Lacks emotional communication skills e.g. Poor listener, interruptive, quick to invalidate, fails to perceive emotions being communicated,

- Focuses on facts rather than feelings

- Does not consider others feelings before acting

- Insecure and defensive – Find it hard to admit mistakes, to express remorse, or sincerely apologize

## Negative effects of low EI

- Social delinquency
- Anxiety and depression
- Attention deficiency
- Aggressiveness
- Bullying
- Poor relationships – Parent-child, teacher-student, therapist-patient, etc

## What are the effects of emotional intelligence?

General emotional intelligence has an effect on the following:

- Performance

- Mental health

- Physical health

- Social health

## Effects of emotional intelligence on your performance

High emotional intelligence can boost your performance both at work and study. Motivation is one key ingredient of high emotional intelligence. With motivation, you can go the extra mile in boosting both work and study performance. On the other hand low emotional intelligence can result in lack of motivation which makes you underperform or even quit performing certain things e.g. quitting studies or quitting work.

## Effect of emotional intelligence on your mental health

Emotions have a great impact on your mental health. Negative emotions, a product of low mental intelligence, are known to wreck havoc on your mental health. They cause stress and, and in extreme cases, depression.

## Effect of emotional intelligence on your physical health

Stress and depression are a product of mental illness due to low emotional intelligence. Both stress and depression have been found out to be leading triggers of high blood pressure, obesity, and diabetes, among other physical health conditions. Studies have also found out that stress and depression suppresses your immune system. A suppressed immune system makes your body more susceptible to infections and diseases.

**Effects on your social health**

Good, positive and productive relationships are a measure of your social health. High emotional intelligence enables you to communicate your feeling in a manner that can be positively perceived and easily understood. This brings about appropriate response to your emotional communication.

On the other hand, high emotional intelligence enables you to properly perceive emotional signals from others. This makes you understand others well. This also enables you to make an appropriate response.

Relationships become healthy when emotional communication is effective and sound. The resultant effect is strengthened bonds, less conflicts (unnecessary emotional noise) and more effort towards attainment of group's social goals.

# THE DIFFERENCE BETWEEN EMOTIONAL QUOTIENT AND INTELLIGENCE QUOTIENT

We have seen in the first Section what emotional intelligence is. The standard used to measure one's emotional intelligence is what is known as Emotional Quotient (EQ). On the other hand, the standard used to measure mental intelligence (or general intelligence as we have traditionally known) is what is famously known as Intelligence Quotient (IQ).

Both EQ and IQ are measuring standards. To be able to distinguish between these two standards, we must first of all be able to distinguish between the two matters that they are measuring. That is, emotional intelligence and mental intelligence.

We have already discussed what emotional intelligence is in our first Section and will continue to expound on it in the rest of this book. Thus we need to briefly discuss what mental intelligence is so that we are on the same platform in terms deriving comparative evaluation.

## What is mental intelligence?

Mental intelligence, otherwise known simply as general intelligence, is a person's capacity to:

1. Acquire knowledge – that is, to learn and understand

2. Apply knowledge – that is, solve problems

3. Engage in abstract reasoning

Thus, it is the power of one's intellect.

## How is IQ derived?

IQ has traditionally been derived as a quotient between one's mental age and one's chronological age factored to an index of 100.

## What factors determines one's IQ

There are several factors that determine one's IQ. These factors fall into two broad categories;

1. Genetic factors
2. Environmental factors

## Genetic factors

These are largely inherent biological factors which are inherited from one's parents. Genetic factors play a much greater role in determining one's IQ.

## Environmental factors

There are several environmental factors that influence one's IQ;

1. Stimulating environment
2. Parental encouragement
3. Good schooling
4. Specific reasoning skills
5. Continued practice
6. Biological factors

There are certain biological factors which result from environment but have a different impact on IQ as they affect biological functioning of the brain. These factors include;

- Pre-natal care
- Proper nutrition
- Absence of disease
- Absence of physical trauma

**Have you wondered why people with high IQ struggle in life while those with moderate IQ succeed?**

Robert Kiyosaki's famous comment is that "... 'A' people work for 'C' people and 'B' people work for the government".

Surprisingly this is the world's reality. 'A' people are mostly the professionals – lawyers, doctors, dentists, engineers, and the like. Most of them own consultancy firms to serve the general public (mostly the 'C' people). It hardly appears to most of them that they are actually employees of the 'C' people rather than their bosses. Yes, without the 'C' people, a bulk of their incomes would not exist.

A bulk of the 'B' people work for the government; some as social workers, some as economic planners, some in various other government functions and departments - just aligned as the various other faculties at the university that admit the 'B' people.

However, what we must not forget that the bulk of taxpayers are the 'C' people. Thus, indirectly 'B' people still work for the 'C' people.

The 'C' people are the entrepreneurs, the businesspeople and those who form a majority of the private sector engines.

Both 'A' and 'B' people are square pegs. They lack all-round creativity. They are relatively high in IQ but relatively low in EQ. On the other hand, the 'C' people are the round pegs. They are endowed with all-round creativity required for enterprises exist and adjust to dynamic environments. Generally, they have average IQ but higher EQ compared to the 'A' and the 'B' people.

Most 'A' and 'B' people hardly prosper beyond their square quarters (consultancies and high-end jobs). On the other hand, 'C' people hardly have square quarters' since the horizon of success is hardly square, 'C' people's perspectives can easily fit to the ends of horizon.

'C' people adjust easier to a new challenging environment than the 'A' and 'B' people. For example, when economic situation gets difficult, a 'C' person can easily start vending sweets, fruits, vegetables, food and such other small things. Most 'A' and 'B' people would rather surrender themselves to alcoholism and suicide to relieve their selves from stress than to accept that they have to start off so low. They are more susceptible to stress and depression. They find it hard to cope with loss of status.

### Exemplified difference between IQ and EQ

Inborn –vs- Acquired

- IQ is inborn by nature (but can be optimized through learning)
- EQ is acquired through learning

Entry –vs- Residence

- IQ enables you to access entry
- EQ enables you to stay in after access

Facts –vs- Reason

- IQ enables one to provide facts as convincing mechanism
- EQ enables one to provide reason as convincing mechanism

Victim –vs- Master

- IQ leaves you a victim of emotions
- EQ enables you to be a master of emotions

Brain –vs- Heart

- IQ enables you to be brain smart
- EQ enables you to be heart smart

School –vs- Life

- IQ enables you to succeed through school
- EQ enables you to succeed through life

Technical –vs- managerial

- IQ enables one to achieve highest levels of technical competence
- EQ enables one to achieve highest levels of leadership competence

Mental -vs- social

- IQ enables one to solve challenges requiring mental ability

- EQ enables one to solve challenges requiring social ability

Technical truth –vs- emotional truth

- IQ enables one to understand what is technically true
- EQ enables one to understand what is emotionally true

**IQ is more static while EQ is more dynamic**

You can easily increase your EQ. However, IQ, though you may optimize it, it is less elastic compared to EQ.

# BENEFITS OF HAVING A HIGH EMOTIONAL INTELLIGENCE

Benefits of high emotional intelligence are immense and unlimited. Nonetheless, we can group them under the following main categories;

1. Emotional control
2. Adaptability
3. Rational decision-making
4. Compassion
5. Optimism
6. Strong bonds
7. Stress management

**Emotional control**

Being in control of your emotions helps you stay calm and rationally query the source of these negative emotions so that you can deal with their root causes. More often than not, we respond to triggers of negative emotions which are only symptoms rather than the disease itself. Through rationalizing our emotions we are able to be less angry by realizing that, probably, the things that trigger our anger are not its root cause.

For example, a parent with low EQ will resort to spanking, beating and brutally punishing his child for small mistakes that children make as part of their learning process. While, if they were emotionally intelligent, they would have realized that the root cause is probably frustrations at work, study or even spousal relationship. It could also be due to harsh economic circumstances.

Lack of emotional control has caused some of the worst crimes in the world. These include;

- Suicide – People who commit suicide mostly suffer from low EQ. Of course, there are exceptions such as mental disease which someone may not be in control or may not have realized its existence. However, most of those who are not suffering from mental illness commit suicide due to low EQ.

- Murder – Most people who commit murder have low EQ. They have kept poisonous negative emotions to accumulate to excessive levels. They sort for revenge or elimination of those who they perceive threats to their goals. In this regard, they murder not necessarily because they have any justification but due to inferiorities caused by their low EQ.

- War – Many leaders who have caused wars within their nations or between their nation and others often suffered from unbridled ego. A deeper look at what caused them to trigger war would reveal their inherent emotional weakness. They suffer from inferiorities due to low EQ and they falsely come to the conclusion that to address their threats (fears), the only remedy is to resort to war. Hitler is a good example of such leaders in history.

- Genocide – Most leaders who have executed genocide have always felt emotionally inferior to those subjects that they have committed genocide against. Thus, to fill the void of their emotional inferiorities, they falsely resort to genocide which they think is the only tool that can enable them get rid of those subjects they feel are a threat to them. Hitler, Stalin and Mao Tse Tung, among others, have been historical examples of such rulers.

## Adaptability

Adaptability is about adjusting yourself to cope with changing situation. People who have high EQ are able to adjust themselves to take advantage of changing circumstances. Those with low EQ get swept away as they cling to the past.

Adaptability is the first and foremost reason why shrewd business entrepreneurs survive in the long-term. It is not about their IQ but rather their EQ. Adaptability breeds creativity and innovation.

Without adaptability one soon becomes irrelevant and his/her past knowledge (acquired through IQ) become obsolete. It is EQ that helps to optimize the benefits of IQ.

## Rational Decision-Making

One major characteristic of people with low EQ is how they make decisions. People with low EQ often make impulse decisions. Such impulse decisions include:

- Impulse buying – This is by far the commonest of all irrational decisions that people with low EQ engage in. They buy things simply because they have become emotionally pulled to them. They are the greatest victims of advertisers and shrewd marketers. They end up buying things that don't meet their needs but wants.

- Impulse consumption – Bingeing is one of the greatest challenges of impulse consumption. People with low EQ resort to eating because they have seen food or simply because others are eating. Not necessarily because they are hungry or it is time to eat. They are controlled by emotional impulses that result into craving habits.

- Impulse quitting – There are those people who are quit everything easily. You cannot pin them to any endeavor that they successfully pulled off to conclusion. They quit jobs because they quarreled with their bosses at work. They quit college simply because they had differences with their lecturers. They quit a journey simply because they couldn't stomach a passenger next to them. Impulse quitting is largely a symptom of low EQ.

## Compassion

Compassion is love expressed through empathy. It is putting yourself in the shoes of those suffering and deciding to do something to relieve their suffering.

Compassion helps to prevent conflicts. It is through compassion that charity organizations exist. It is through compassion that disaster relief works. It is through compassion that the plight of the vulnerable and disadvantaged in society is taken care of.

Compassion is the glue that binds and sustains relationships.

## Optimism

Optimism is a product of self-confidence. Self-confidence arises from one's Self-Esteem. On the other hand, self-esteem is derived from one's positive mental image.

If you have a mental image that projects you as a failure, weak and incapable, then, you are more likely going to suffer from low self-esteem. You will be less optimistic about your chances of success in whichever endeavor that you take.

On the other hand, if you have positive mental image of yourself such that you see yourself as successful, and very strong, then, you are going have higher self-esteem. This high self-esteem will boost your self-confidence. With self-confidence you become optimistic about your chances of success in whichever endeavor you take.

## Strong bonds

Studies have found out that people with higher EQ are able to form interpersonal relationships and easily fit into groups.

Relationships are sustained by EQ. A higher EQ means that you are more compassionate towards others since you are empathetic enough to understand their situation. This way, you are able to serve them and support them.

Strong bonds are about service and sacrifice. Strong ego, which is a product of low EQ, makes one indifferent and too proud to think of serving others. It makes one less inclined to sacrifice for the benefit of helping others. This weakens bonds. This creates poor relationships.

## Stress management

Stress is one of the greatest consequences of low EQ. Yes, not all forms of stress are caused by low EQ, but, most of them are. You can significantly cut on your stress levels by simply boosting your EQ Levels.

Studies have found that people with higher EQ are able to understand their own psychological state and thus easily cope with stress and avoid depression. They have also found out that people with high EQ are much happier than those with low EQ as they suffer less from stress. They are able to adapt and cope with challenges, be they at school, at work or in relationships.

# REAL LIFE EXAMPLES OF EMOTIONAL INTELLIGENCE

Most successful leaders of all time have always alluded to the most enduring quality of success, PERSISTENCE. They more than often alluded that the persistent people reach levels where the geniuses can never ever dare to reach.

As we have seen from our previous discussions, persistence is one of the greatest qualities of people with higher EQ. This is achieved because they are highly adaptable, thus, being able to adjust to suit changing circumstances in order to achieve their goals. Therefore, people with high EQ are more resilient in their pursuits.

This position has been supported by many research findings. Most studies have come to establish that IQ only contributes to between 20% to 25% of your success. EQ contributes the remaining 75% to 80% of your success.

One important point that must not be overlooked is that you cannot substitute IQ with EQ. Both are needed. IQ is the foundation upon which you build your EQ. Thus, without IQ, EQ cannot exist. Yet, without EQ, you can hardly soar to greater heights of success.

Also, as we shall find, and as previously alluded, IQ enables you to succeed in school. Yet, it is EQ that enables you to succeed in life. Thus, in post-schooling, EQ takes prominence in your everyday success.

In this section we are going to consider some real life examples of emotional intelligence at place in the five main domains of life;

- Home
- Work
- Study
- Relationships
- leadership

## Real life example of emotional intelligence at home

"A little boy, out of pride (and some sense of generosity), takes the cake his mom had bought as a birthday surprise to her visiting sister. The child shares out this with her friends and they enjoy it all. Mum discovers there is no cake when she wants to keep it near the dining table. This is just after receiving a call from her sister who says she has arrived at the airport.

Out of anger, mum beats her son in a brutal way. The son bleeds to unconsciousness. Ambulance is called and mum gets to hospital with her son...."

Yes, this is just a depiction of some sad stories that happen in some homes across the world. The consequences of not controlling one's impulses make a big mountain out of an ant-hill. Situations where parents have inadvertently killed their young ones while punishing them are common. Had they resorted to using their EQ, they would have controlled their emotional impulses and reasoned enough to have the most appropriate discipline that doesn't cause disaster.

For example, in this scenario, the mother should have probably calmed herself and, since, the cake was a surprise, just forgot about it since her sister would not have really known about what happened. Yes, how can you tell a surprise if it was really a surprise? The boy and his niece would have enjoyed the occasion. Later on, after the sister is gone, that would be the moment to hold the boy to account.

As a result of acting on impulses, her sister misses both of them at home. She is forced to wait. After getting tired of waiting, she goes to hospital to visit the boy in the most unfortunate situation. The boy is still unconscious. Later on, the boy dies from internal bleeding. An occasion of joy turns somber simply because of emotional impulses.

The world is full of such bad occurrences.

## Why is EQ important at home?

Domestic violence accounts for the bulk of cases where low EQ is involved. Brutality against children is the commonest, though brutality between spouses is the one that commonly reaches the public knowledge. Siblings fighting each other due to simple misunderstandings is also another common factor due to low EQ.

Parents with high EQ minimize conflicts at home. They help improve their children's EQ by teaching them the importance of empathy. They help them to learn compassion by showing them how to donate and help others in difficult situations. This also helps parents enforce empathy and compassion towards their children so they avoid cruel punishment when their children go wrong.

## Real life example of emotional intelligence at work

A Sales Manager furiously confronts the Receptionist as to why she didn't inform her that her friend called. A visitor is seated on the reception couch. The visitor tries to intervene as the Sales Manager gets nasty. The Sales manager angrily tells the visitor "get out this, it doesn't concern you". The Receptionists smartly tries to excuse the situation by interjecting "Dear Boss, I am sorry. Have you been expecting someone?" The Sales Manager responds "Yes, very respectable person" as she stares at the visitor in a derogatory way. The visitor replies "thank you for letting me know" and he walks out.

The Sales Manager goes back to her office. She waits for about an hour for her "very respectable person". Pensively, she goes back to the receptionist and asks "Did you really book an appointment with that important client that I have been waiting for? Do you know that he has an important deal that we must get or else I have no job?" The Reception simply replies "He is that visitor who walked away the last moment you were here".

This is among the many scenarios that take place in our workplaces. It is much more penalizing when a superior member of staff loses out on EQ over a junior staff member. For it is more difficult for a junior staff to correct his superior than for a superior to correct his junior. This is why senior staff attend more EQ seminars and orientations than their juniors. This is so that they can not only boost their EQ but also help their juniors.

In the above scenario, the Sales Manager, instead of using her EQ, tried to prove her superiority. In the end she lost an important client. The company lost a multi-million deal as this client wanted to experience the feel of the organization from inside as the deal was sensitive and required a lot of soft skills. The client explains to the company director what happened as the reason why he is backing off the deal. The director fires her Sales Manager.

There are many challenging situations at work. Some are more serious that this. People are becoming increasingly sensitive as to how they are treated. Thus, soft skills have jumped to the forefront of determining whether a firm will have a competitive edge or not. Employees are required to acquire these soft skills to navigate firms to their competitive edge.

A recent study conducted by Human Resources consultancy found out that 67% of all competencies required for success at work place are EQ related;

- EQ helps you to easily get internships

- EQ enables you to easily climb the ladder to become an administrator

- IQ gets you hired, but it is EQ that decides whether you will be retained, fired or promoted.

## Negative effects of low EQ at workplace

A study conducted in a work environment has shown that low EQ behaviors at workplace such as moodiness, incivility, angry outbursts and rude comments are responsible for stress, burnouts and anxious work environments.

The study found out the following about these low EQ behaviours;

- 12% of employees resigned as a result of low EQ behavior
- 4/5 of employees wasted work time worrying about a low EQ behavioral incident
- 2/3 employees reported declined performance due to a low EQ environment
- 63% of employees wasted time avoid their low EQ offenders
- More than ¾ of employees reported waning commitment to their employer because of low EQ environment

The following were established as some of the characteristics of High EQ work environments:

- Use of humor as a strategy for project success
- Effective communication
- High levels of collaboration
- High morale
- High levels of job and company engagement

The resultant positive impact in High EQ work environments registered:

- High levels of job satisfaction
- Increased employee tenure
- Higher productivity
- Boosted bottom-line

Poor EI employees cause:

- High rate of absenteeism
- Lowered productivity (due to poor team work)
- Lost revenue (due to poor customer service)
- Loss of wealth (due to loss of profitability)

Why have those employees with higher EQ been found to perform better than those with higher IQ?

1. They are more aware of themselves – Being aware of oneself makes it easy for one to be purpose-oriented. Thus, one is able to achieve higher levels of performance without necessarily being motivated by inducements such as promotion, status, power, etc. Eventually, one gets these not as a target but as benevolent rewards.

2. They are better at regulating themselves – Regulating oneself makes it easy not to upset others, especially one's superiors/supervisors. This breeds good relationship with one's superiors, which is naturally a precondition to not just retaining one's job but receiving promotion.

3. They are good at owning responsibility – Owning responsibility makes one to be able to remain focused on achieving goals and hence easy to admit mistakes.

Admitting mistakes allows one to take control measures necessary for corrective action.

4. They are more motivated – Those who are not motivated can hardly meet their goals.

5. Have greater compassion and empathy towards others – This allows them to easily manage teams, get higher group approval and naturally become better candidates for promotion.

## Real life example of emotional intelligence at study

In a certain boy's school, there are two teachers, Mr. John and Ms. Diana. Mr. John is a tall, heavily built militant-looking man. On the other hand, Ms. Diana is a short, slender and ever smiling girlish teacher.

Both are mathematics teachers and heads of their respective classes. Mr. John, nicknamed as "John Bull" by his students, scored high grades in both high school and college compared to Ms. Diana who is fondly nicknamed "Lady Joy" by her students.

When it comes to their classes, John's class appears to have higher rate of discipline than Diana's class. Everyone is quiet in his class when he is in. He demands performance and reprimands those who fail. Every student is immersed in his books and hardly ask any asks him questions; with no debating.

He is the only voice and any other voice is only heard when some student is responding to his questions.

In Diana's class students appear to be so engaged in debating with each other and asking her questions. There is a lively environment and sometimes a stranger may feel that she has lost control of her class. Diana doesn't punish any student for failing exams, but she does advices those who have failed and seeking from them how they need help. She inspires them to aim high by giving stories of successful people who worked hard and prospered despite being in situations like them.

The above scenario depicts Mr. John, a high IQ teacher who focuses on IQ and demands the same from his students. He has created a strict serious learning environment. It also depicts Ms. Diana, a high EQ teacher who focuses on letting students feel at ease by creating a relaxed learning environment.

Outside classes, John's student leads in acts of bullying and indiscipline. At home they are the most reported by parents as not being keen on doing homework or studying. On the other hand, Diana's students are playful, jovial, less aggressive, and incidences of bullying are rare.

Performance-wise, the average mathematics performance score in Ms. Diana's class has been higher than that of Mr. John.

The outcome in terms' class performance and outside class behavior would be expected to favor Mr. John. However, contrary to ordinary expectations, they favor Ms. Diana. Why? This is the effect of high EQ on the part of Diana which she has also served to boost in her students. Mr. John, with a proven higher IQ than Ms. Diana, has focused less on boosting his student's EQ for he has not worked on his own.

In a bid to find out why Mr. John's students are more indisciplined outside class environment compared to Ms. Diana's students, despite Mr. John being a strict disciplinarian, the administration interrogated an equal number of students from each class. They found out that most of Mr. John's students had low regard of him and did find little that they could emulate from him outside the classroom. On the other hand, Ms. Diana's students had very high regard of her and could quickly list so many things worth emulating from her outside classroom. They were also more motivated than Mr. John's students.

## IQ –vs- EQ in schools

Learning institutions are places where IQ is the most emphasized form of intelligence. However, recent findings have discovered that EQ helps boost one's IQ-related activities. Thus, in most schools, students are taught on how to acquire and understand factual knowledge.

However, they are not taught on how to handle stress, anxiety, failure, burnout, inferiority complex, ego issues, etc. They are also not taught how to manage our emotions.

Schools that register high performance levels in terms of well-rounded students are those that have been able to appreciate the importance of EQ; and thus balanced out between IQ and EQ needs.

## Real life example of emotional intelligence in relationships

Ronald was married to Elizabeth, and their marriage was happy. They were both professional Engineers. It seemed a happy marriage at start. However, after 6 months of marriage, things had gotten pretty rocky. Ronald accused Elizabeth of aloofness. On the other hand, Elizabeth accused Ronald of angry outbursts. By 11th month, they dissolved their marriage due to irreconcilable differences.

In this scenario, both Ronald and Elizabeth had reasonably high IQ. However, aloofness on the side of Elizabeth was her lows in terms of EQ. On the other hand, Ronald's angry outbursts were his undoing in terms of EQ.

Had Ronald considered taking control of his emotional outbursts, he would have probably helped Elizabeth to learn aloofness isn't great. On the other hand, had Elizabeth not resorted to aloofness and kept engaging Ronald in such a manner that would help Ronald realize his folly, probably, marriage could have been saved.

Ronald eventually got remarried to Mercy. Mercy was a social worker who didn't get to university. After four months of their marriage, Ronald resorted to his ways - emotional outbursts. Mercy endured for a while but by the 7th month of marriage Ronald had became too unbearable despite Mercy's best effort. Mercy realized she had to change tact. She started attending psychological counseling herself, reached out to Ronald's friends and siblings. This drew support on her side. She eventually convinced Ronald to start attending psychological counseling four months after desperate attempts.

Psychologist revealed that Ronald was suffering from effects of early childhood trauma. His mother was alcoholic and emotionally abusive to him. It seems he had this kind of revenge on her which he projected to his wives. It took three months of psychological counseling and Ronald was able to overcome his childhood trauma and the emotional outbursts ceased. Fourteen years down the line, a marriage that was almost breaking up after 7 months has not only endured for all these years but is growing much stronger and both partners are living happily.

As it can be seen, Mercy had a higher EQ than Elizabeth. She took up the challenge. She stepped into Ronald's shoes and compassionately sought to help him. She eventually managed to uplift Ronald. The end reward is a happy marriage.

It can also be seen that Ronald wasn't emotionally intelligent enough to become self-aware of the root cause of his emotional outbursts. He kept blaming his wives instead of seeking to explore the root cause of his troubles. It took a woman with higher EQ than him to solve his problem.

**Impact of EQ on Relationships**

EQ has been found to be the glue that binds relationships. Many marriages are failing today because people are mechanically seeking partners whose IQ matches as opposed to EQ. While the matching IQ makes them feel great, their relationship never lasts. Those few who put EQ matching as a priority end up not only with a more lasting marriage but also a happier one.

EQ helps to prevent conflicts, addresses root cause of potential conflicts and make partners adapt to each other and their changing circumstances.

**What are the qualities of a leader with high EQ?**

A leader who has high EQ;

- Makes great decisions

- Will understand people

- Creates a conducive atmosphere

- Build trust by showing sensitivity to people's needs and situations

- Combine emotional energy and enthusiasm to motivate others while tempering negative responses to distressing situations

**IQ –vs- EQ mix in leadership**

As we said earlier, IQ is irreplaceable. Thus, as a leader you must have some reasonable level of IQ. However, EQ has a great impact in making you a better leader than others.

The following is the IQ –vs- EQ mix percentage in terms the key leadership factors;

- Goal setting – 30/70

- Decision-making – 50/50
- Communication – 10/90
- Motivation & inspiration – 05/95
- Team work – 40/60
- Time management – 30/70

As can be seen, it is only in decision-making where both IQ and EQ balance out. In the rest of leadership factors, EQ supersedes IQ.

# HOW TO TEST YOUR EMOTIONAL INTELLIGENCE

Testing your emotional intelligence is one of the best ways to tell whether you have a good EQ or you need to make some improvements.

There are many EQ tests that have emerged of late. However not all are empirically tested and thus cannot be relied upon for accuracy. Thus, you need to be careful about which is genuine or which one is not.

Consortium for Research on Emotional Intelligence In Organizations (CREIO) is an organization comprising or entities dedicated in the field of research on emotional intelligence.

CREIO recommends the following EI testing tools as empirically proven;

- Emotional & Social Competence Inventory
- Emotional and Social Competence Inventory - U
- BarOn Emotional Quotient Inventory
- Schutte Self Report EI Test
- Wong's Emotional Intelligence Scale
- Mayer-Salovey-Caruso EI Test (MSCEIT)
- Genos Emotional Intelligence Inventory
- Work Group Emotional Intelligence Profile

- Trait Emotional Intelligence Questionnaire (TEIQue)
- Group Emotional Competency Inventory

For in-depth information on each of these tools and how to apply them, please visit Consortium for Research on Emotional Intelligence In Organizations (CREIO).

# HOW TO IMPROVE YOUR EMOTIONAL INTELLIGENCE

Unlike IQ, which extremely static and slow to adjust, EQ is extremely dynamic and elastically adjustable. This makes it practically easy to improve your emotional intelligence.

## How do you boost your emotional intelligence?

To boost your emotional intelligence, you need to build the following key skills

1. Self-awareness skills

2. Self-management skills

3. Social-awareness skills

4. Social-management (relationship management) skills

The following are some of the ways by which you can boost your emotional intelligence:

## Build your self-awareness skills;

- Tap into your emotions (self-awareness). Note and record your emotional reactions to key events in your day

- Listen to your body. Note how you behave in response to your emotions.

- Observe the correlation between your emotions and your behaviors.

## Build your self-management skills

- Detach your mind from the expressions of your emotions.

- Examine your emotional trend.

- Decouple your behavior from your negative emotions.

## Build your social-awareness skills

- Be open-minded

- Boost your empathy and compassion

- Master people's body language

- Explore the effect you have on others

- Practice emotional honesty

## Build your social-management skills

Social management skills are simply relationship management skills. It is about managing how you relate with others. Your competence in managing relationships is what is commonly known as **social competence**.

## Practicing as the best way to empower your emotional intelligence

Just like IQ, practice boosts the optimal use of your emotional intelligence. Unlike IQ that is less elastic, EQ is extremely responsive to practice. By practicing, you not only optimize your EQ utility but also expand its capacity.

## Strategies to counter your low emotional intelligence

The following are 5 key strategies to counter your low EQ and hence contribute to improving your emotional intelligence:

1. Get feedback – Feedback from people, more so your friends and loved ones can enable you to learn their perception about your EQ

2. Beware of the gap between intent and impact – When you utter a word or act in a certain way, try to imagine its impact on others. You may crack a joke that you deliberately intend to poke another person, but without imagining its impact, you may end up hurting and dampening spirits instead of lighting up the moment.

3. Master how to make a pause – Whenever responding to people's emotions, it is always good to pause. This gives you an opportunity to think. At the same time, it gives the other party an opportunity to reflect. Both ways, it helps to mitigate the severity of negative outcomes.

4. Master how to redirect after a pause – Once you've paused and realized that your approach hasn't been positive, how you redirect your approach matters. Find a less pervasive approach. If possible, postpone the subject at hand to a fairer time or switch to another less divisive subject.

5. Wear both shoes – Always put yourself in the shoes of the person you are engaging with. This helps to reduce the gap between your intent and impact.

## How to raise your EQ

The following are general ways to raise your EQ;

1. Knowing one's emotions

   - Recognize how you feel and identify and label each feeling

   - Understand why you feel that way

- Distinguish between feelings and actions

2. Motivating oneself

   - Productively harness your feelings

   - Practice emotional self-control

   - Delay gratification until you achieve your goals

3. Recognizing other people's emotions

   - Be sensitive to other people's emotions

4. Managing your emotions

   - Understand one's feelings

   - Balance between over-sensitivity and emotional suppression

5. Managing relationships

   - Be perceptive

   - Resolve conflicts rather than ignoring them

   - Be considerate and co-operative

**Further tips on improving your EQ (more so, at workplace)**

- Understand the root cause of your feelings

- Know your frustration tolerance

- Express your anger in the most appropriate way (not to hurt or victimize but to make your feelings known)

- Monitor your actions

- Work with your strengths

- Focus attention on improving your EQ

- Nurture self-esteem

- Keep off self-destructive behaviors

- Stabilize your emotions through mindfulness meditation

# DAILY HABITS TO IMPROVE YOUR EMOTIONAL INTELLIGENCE

Habits are repetitive ways of doing things. Habits are important in our daily lives as they enable us keep routines.

The following are the 30 daily habits you can practice to improve your emotional intelligence;

1.  Meditate often and much – Meditation is your mind's tonic. It relieves your mind from the extreme vibration of razing thoughts. You are able de-clutter your mind and focus attention. Meditation is your mind's sweeping broom.

2.  Practice mindfulness – Mindfulness is a mental attitude and posture that enables you to become self-ware of the present moment. It helps you to avoid being dragged by thoughts of the past. It helps you be aware of negative thoughts without attaching to them;.It helps you to avoid negative thoughts about the future which brings worry. Without regrets and worries, you fully live in the present. You fully utilize it. You get fully attentive to your emotional energy. You don't react based on your past or future. You are able to overcome stress and thus depression. You are able to detect, monitor and manage

your emotional impulses. And, you are more composed regardless of the turbulence of the moment.

3. Practice compassion – Compassion is a love in action. It is a love triggered by empathy, that is concern for others. Compassion can be expressed by visiting the sick; helping those in calamities; donating to those in dire need of material help such as food, clothing and shelter; sharing time and presence with the lonely; taking care of the children and the elderly in their homes, among so many others. Compassion shapes your attitude. Compassion boosts your positive emotional energy. Compassion helps you to cut down on your pride and ego. Compassion helps you to remove greed from your heart. Compassion humbles you. Compassion increases your EQ level

4. Balance between work and play – The dullest people are those who have no time to play. Dullness is a sign that your intelligence is operating sub-optimally, more so, your emotional intelligence. Thus, to light up that bulb of emotional intelligence that has been dimmed due to low energy, you need to play and exercise. The energy will rise up to brighten it. You obviously will gain the joys of it. The

energy of your joys will be radiated into others and a happy bond will develop.

5. Be curious about others – Being curious is not about being suspicious. It is simply about being keen and interested in knowing others. Have that curious attitude and develop that curious posture. This helps others know that you have interest in them and their wellbeing.

6. Accept your imperfections – Never ever assume a perfect posture. Be humane and humble enough to submit that you are an imperfect being. Thus, whatever position you take, or whatever statement you make, don't assume that it is error-free. This way, you can positively respond to criticism from others.

7. Accept others as they are – Don't try to change others. Don't try to convince others. Don't try to overly persuade them. Simply inspire them. But, before you can possibly inspire anyone, you must first understand and accept who the person is. Convincing and persuading are externally driven efforts. Inspiring is internally driven effort. In inspiring, you are not lighting the fire outside the person, but, on the contrary, you are igniting inner flames within the person.

8. Improve your motivation – Motivation is what drives you. Cultivate a positive mindset. This will help you have a winning attitude. It is a winning attitude that drives you towards achieving your goals.

9. Keep safe boundaries – Yes, avoid psychic vampires. Psychic vampires are those people who, no matter what, deflates your emotional energy.

10. Be more proactive and less reactive – To be proactive is to anticipate a likely situation and prepare for it in advance rather than wait for it to occur and react to it. Listen to your instincts. Learn what happens in possible circumstances that you are about to deal with. Map out a "what if" scenario and lay out appropriate responses. This will help you avoid negative impulsive reactions.

11. Practice intimacy – Learning to practice the right kind of intimacy to different kind of people helps you to strengthen bonds. Intimacy is simply body connection enabled through sensory cues. Touch intimacy (e.g. hug, pat, kiss, greetings, etc), eye intimacy (e.g. gazing, squinting, etc), scent (e.g. rose fragrance, etc); seductive words (e.g. poem, song, speech, story, etc) can help

enhance intimacy. However, there is nothing as offensive as wrong intimacy signal. So, learn and respect people's age, culture, profession, status, religion, gender, etc.

12. Boost your bouncing mechanism – Ability to bounce back from adversity

13. Practice assertiveness – Be firm yet polite

14. Practice positive thinking – Positive thinking is simply the art of turning negative thoughts into positive thoughts. It is finding the positive side of every negative thing. Just as a shadow means that the opposite end has a source of light so do negative thoughts, negative occurrences or negative people have their positive side.

15. Occupy your mind with more inspirational materials – Read inspirational content, tell inspirational stories, etc. Learn to tell positive stories. Practice reading and listening to inspirational content. All these helps to shape your attitude. You end up with a more positive attitude which boosts your positive self-image, increases your self-esteem and improves your self-confidence and assertiveness.

16. Always pause when angered or when argument becomes heated.

17. Always ask other people's perspectives – It is always important to remember that not all people respond by expressing their mind about certain issues. Thus, it is necessary to ask their perspectives. This will help to lower their resistance to your point of view. It will also help to avoid rebellion. Also, asking for people's perspective to their point of view enables you to know their feelings and emotional state.

18. Respectfully disagree – There will always be disagreements. This is the beauty of diversity. However, what turns disagreement into nasty affair is loss of respect to the rules of engagement. Most disagreements are about issues. Don't personalize and start attacking the personality of the one you are disagreeing with. Respect someone's personality and stay on the issue.

19. Stick to mantra that resonates with you – A mantra is a cue word that you keep repeating to remind yourself or reinforce a certain thought or action. For example, "rise above them" is an easy mantle that can help you stay safe from heated argument or angry outbursts. When someone engages in emotional outbursts such as verbal insults, that means their EQ has gone low. When you silently repeat the

mantra "rise above them", you are simply rallying yourself to raise your EQ level so that you don't resort to insulting back or overreacting. Another great mantra provided by Michelle Obama is "when they go low, we go high". This offers a positive challenge on how you should respond to those who go low in terms of EQ.

20. Reflect on your emotional responses at the end of the day – So many times, you may not realize your faults the moment you are expressing your emotions. Later in the day, while your mind is at rest, it becomes easier to reflect back and establish whether your behavior was appropriate or not. Practicing that can accelearate your learning of emotions and thus boost your EQ.

21. Assume the best intent in others – Never premeditate negative intents in others. Always wish the best intents in others. This way, you can avoid overreacting to their negative comments or negative body language. Also, it enables you to consider the possibility that some of the negative signals could be "noisy" signals, that is, unintended signals. However, this does not necessarily mean that you suppress your instincts. Take note of your instincts as positive alarms that you need to be more observant and more careful. Instincts can help you avoid danger.

22. Exercise daily in the morning – Exercising in the morning helps to set positive mood for the day. This also boosts your brain's oxygen intake thus minimizing stress. It also helps to release 'happy hormones' which enables you have a radiance of 'feel good' effect.

23. Breathe before you speak – Breathing is one of the best ways to release tension. Breathing before you speak releases accumulated negative energy. It also enables you to be in control of your body language e.g. tremor, shaking, harsh tone, etc, which could be signs of uncontrollable anger or fear.

24. Encourage criticism – Criticism, whether positive or negative helps one to learn. You can learn both the information in the message and the intent behind the message. A positive intent means that person cares for you, irrespective of whether the criticism is positive or negative, though, negative criticism, if persistent could point to an adversary. Encourage positive criticism and learn what is being conveyed. Criticism is the most important feedback you need so as to take a corrective action on your EQ.

25. Be honest with yourself – Don't find excuses for your emotional failures. Accept them as part of your learning process. If you are feeling jealous, accept it. Don't deflect it for it will grow into a monstrous outcome.

26. Give back to society (compassion) – Join charity organizations to volunteer during your free time. Participate in corporate social responsibility. Be concerned about the welfare of the unfortunate.

27. Communicate with awareness (mindful communication) – e.g. be aware of your vocals and other emotional cues.

28. Manage your stress – Carry out those activities and diets that can help you be free of stress.

29. Give gratitude – Acknowledge and reward good behaviors. Appreciate others for doing good to you. Appreciate the good things that you have in life.

30. Observe those around you – Each person is different. Different people are triggered by different emotional cues. Learn those positive cues that inspires each of your relationships. Also learn those negative cues that discourage some. Practice the positive cues as you avoid the negative ones.

## Tips on do's

- Take time everyday to appreciate that which is good in others

- Take time everyday to appreciate the abundance of goodness around you

- Increase your emotional word vocabulary

- Be your own best friend

- Listen with your heart

- Talk back to yourself

- Tune into your body

- Smile more and often

## Tips on don'ts

- Never speak out of anger

- Never act out of fear

- Never choose from impatience

# CONCLUSION

Thank you for acquiring this book and reading it to the end.

This book has provided important information you need to know about emotional intelligence. It has also provided practical benefits and hands-on techniques that can enable you to improve your emotional intelligence so that you can be smart in life, earn greater rewards and live happily.

It is my sincere hope that this guide has enabled you to learn and understand what emotional intelligence is and worked to improved it to enjoy its immense benefits. It is also my sincere hope that you have been able to share with others information gathered in this book, techniques you have applied and your experiences with others. I humbly request that you encourage others to acquire this book so that it can be their companion while practicing and exploring more on emotional intelligence.

Again, thank you for acquiring and reading this book.

Good luck!